Money Matters Sorted

Daniel Jones

Copyright © 2023 Daniel Jones

All rights reserved.

No part of this publication may be reproduced, distributed, or transmitted in any form or by any means, including photocopying, recording, or other electronic or mechanical methods, without the prior written permission of the author, except in the case of brief quotations embodied in critical reviews and certain other non-commercial uses permitted by copyright law.

Independently Published on Amazon

ISBN: (Paperback) 9798320136448

Also available on Amazon as an ebook

Image credits:

Tobias Walker www.tobias-walker.com

Table of Contents

Introduction 1

Chapter 1: Building a Strong Financial Foundation 5

Chapter 2: Understanding Money Basics 11

Chapter 3: Managing Your Money Wisely 19

Chapter 4: Saving Strategies for a Brighter Future 27

Chapter 5: The Power of Smart Spending 33

Chapter 6: Credit and Debt: Making Informed Choices 37

Chapter 7: Exploring the World of Investments 45

Chapter 8: Navigating the Job Market: Career and Income 55

Chapter 9: Entrepreneurship - Turning Ideas into Financial Success 63

Chapter 10: Giving Back - Philanthropy and Community Impact 73

Conclusion 81

Timeline of Tips 85

About the Author 91

Introduction

Welcome to the world of financial education, where knowledge and understanding pave the path to a prosperous future. In this book, we embark on a journey through the intricacies of finance, aiming to equip you with the essential tools and insights necessary to make informed decisions about your financial well-being.

In an age where financial systems and markets are constantly evolving, it has become increasingly vital for young people to grasp the **fundamentals** of personal finance. The landscape of money management is evolving rapidly, with new technologies, investment opportunities, and financial products emerging at a staggering pace. Without a solid understanding of these concepts, people can find themselves vulnerable to financial challenges and setbacks.

Financial education is not solely about accumulating wealth, it is also about developing a mindset that promotes financial stability and security. By building a strong foundation of financial knowledge, you can make smarter choices, avoid common pitfalls, and create a solid framework for achieving long-term goals.

Throughout this book, we will explore various topics, from budgeting and saving to investing and retirement planning to volunteering and entrepreneurship. Each chapter delves into key aspects of personal finance, providing clear explanations and real-life examples to illustrate how these concepts apply to everyday life. By connecting theory with practice, you will gain a deeper understanding of the underlying principles and learn how to apply them in practical ways.

By adopting a proactive approach to financial education, you will gain the ability to seize opportunities, protect yourself from unexpected setbacks, and ultimately take control of your financial destiny. This book aims to empower you with the tools necessary to break free from financial stress and embrace a future filled with financial freedom.

I realise that the world of finance can sometimes appear intimidating or overwhelming, but I will try to demystify complex concepts and simplify the language of money. Whether you're a complete novice or already have some financial knowledge, I will give you confidence to step forth and conquer the world of money.

Financial education extends beyond individuals; it also impacts families, communities, and society as a whole. By equipping ourselves with financial literacy, we can create a ripple effect that spreads prosperity and empowers future generations to make better financial choices. When we understand how to manage our money wisely, we become better equipped to support our loved ones, contribute to charitable causes, and build a more financially resilient society.

The benefits of financial education go far beyond just monetary gain. It can provide a sense of security, peace of mind, and the freedom to pursue passions and dreams. It allows you to make choices based on your values, rather than being limited by financial constraints. Financial education is about aligning your financial decisions with your personal goals and aspirations, ensuring that your money becomes a tool for creating the life you desire.

Remember, financial **education** is a lifelong journey, and this book is just the beginning. As you progress through the chapters and absorb the knowledge presented, we encourage you to apply what you learn and continue exploring additional resources to deepen your understanding of personal finance. Seek out reputable financial experts, attend seminars or workshops, and engage in conversations with others who share your interest in financial education. The more you learn, the more empowered you will become.

Now let's embark on this exciting journey together, as we unlock the mysteries of finance and arm ourselves with the knowledge needed to build a brighter financial future. Get ready to transform your relationship with money, elevate your financial literacy, and take control of your financial destiny. Let's dive in!

Money Matters Sorted

Chapter 1: Building a Strong Financial Foundation

Start now...

Buckle up, because we're about to embark on a thrilling journey into the world of financial literacy. Financial literacy is having the knowledge to apply sound financial beliefs to your own money. You might be thinking, "Why on earth is this stuff important?" Grasping finances is having a secret weapon in your pocket. It's all about understanding money and how it works, so you can avoid being bamboozled by sneaky financial traps and make smarter decisions.

Starting early is key. While your friends are busy cluelessly swiping their credit cards and buying things they don't need, you'll be sitting pretty, armed with **knowledge**. By learning the ropes of personal finance from an early age, you'll be well-equipped to handle real-life money situations.

The benefits of starting early cannot be underestimated, they'll make your piggy bank do flick-flaks. You'll develop savvy budgeting skills that will make your future-self proud. Plus, when it comes to saving, you'll have Jedi-like discipline that'll help you achieve your goals faster than your friends, who are still trying to figure out what the difference is between a savings and current account.

Oh, and let's not forget about the sweet taste of financial independence. By getting a head start on financial stuff, you'll learn how to make your money work for you. Investments, **compound interest**, and all those fancy things will become your allies in building wealth. While others are scrambling to catch up, you'll be sipping cocktails on a tropical beach, thanks to your early start in the world of financial wizardry.

In conclusion, my money-smart enthusiasts, financial literacy is your golden ticket to a brighter future. So, embrace its importance with open arms, because starting early is the secret ingredient that will make your financial journey oh-so-sweet. Get ready to conquer the world of money and show everyone that you're the master of your financial domain!

I want a Ferrari by the age of 30

Let's talk about the important world of goal setting. Setting financial goals is stating to your inner-self, " that I'm the manager of my money!" It gives you a clear target to aim for and helps you stay focused on your financial journey. So, grab your favourite pen and get ready to unleash the power of goal setting!

Instilling financial values is like giving your money a spa day. It's all about nurturing healthy habits that will make your wallet jump for joy.

When you learn the value of saving, budgeting, and making wise financial choices, you become a money magician. You'll have the power to make your cash grow and avoid those pesky money monsters that try to steal your hard-earned dough.

Imagine you're on a quest to save for that dream holiday or the latest gaming console.

Without a goal, it's like wandering through a maze without a map. But fear not! Setting financial goals is like activating your GPS to guide you through the money maze. It gives you a sense of direction, helps you prioritise your spending, and makes your money dance to your tune.

In a nutshell, goal setting and instilling financial values are the turbo boosters to financial success. They transform your money journey into an exhilarating adventure. With clear goals

Money Matters Sorted

and strong values, you'll have the power to make smart choices, build wealth, and create the life you've always dreamed of.

Are we allowed to talk about money?

Right, listen up! If you want to avoid turning your family into a bunch of tight-lipped money misers, it's time to embrace the joy of open communication about money. Yes, I know it sounds positively thrilling, doesn't it? So how is it possible to make those money conversations as entertaining as a cricket match?

First things first, you need to create a safe space for these financial confessions. No judgement allowed! Make sure everyone knows that sharing their money matters won't result in banishment to the Tower of London. Encourage open dialogue, listen attentively, and resist the urge to roll your eyes when Aunt Edna brings up her excessive shoe collection.

Nothing says "fun family time" like a good old-fashioned financial meeting. Block out some quality time for these chats, just like you would for afternoon tea. Whip out your best British accent and use phrases like "We shall convene every month to discuss our financial triumphs and tribulations." It's posh, it's proper, and it's bound to get everyone excited about balancing their books.

To keep things interesting, why not introduce a financial game night. Yes, you heard me correctly. Gather the family around

the Monopoly board and unleash your inner money mogul. Use the game as a way to discuss financial concepts, like investing in properties or avoiding bankruptcy. But remember, no throwing the dice at each other when someone lands on Mayfair.

Last but not least, don't forget to sprinkle a dash of humour into these money conversations. After all, laughter is the best seasoning for any financial discussion. Crack jokes about your never-ending pursuit of a bargain or the time Dad accidentally bought an inflatable unicorn for the garden on eBay, thinking it was a real unicorn. Humour helps lighten the mood and makes those potentially dull money talks a tad more bearable.

Let's embrace the art of open **communication** about money with a stiff upper lip and a wink. Foster an environment where money matters are discussed openly, add a touch of charm, and watch as your family becomes the talk of the town with their financial wit and wisdom.

Chapter 2: Understanding Money Basics

Money, my friends, is the magical stuff that makes the world go round. Imagine a world where we had to barter for everything we wanted. "Hey, I'll give you three chickens for that new phone!" Well, money moved the world on from a bartering economy (and to save us from awkward exchanges) by providing a universal way to trade stuff.

Top of the tree is Cash, the rockstar of payments. It's cold, hard, and always ready to rock 'n' roll. Coins jingle in your pocket, and banknotes make you feel like a baller when you whip them out to pay. Cash is perfect for those moments when you need a quick fix of purchasing power.

Cards, my peeps, are the fancy siblings of cash. They're sleek, futuristic gadgets that fit right in your wallet. Debit cards and credit cards are the cool kids on the block. With a debit card, you can spend whatever you have in your bank account, while credit cards give you the power to buy now and pay later (with interest, mind you). Just be careful not to go on a wild spending spree and end up with a credit card bill that could rival the national debt of a small country (discussed in detail in Chapter 6).

Ah, digital payments, the unicorns of money! These little wizards have transformed the way we handle our finances. With digital payments, you can wave goodbye to the hassle of carrying wads of cash or rummaging through your bag to find your card. Just a few taps on your smartphone, and voila! You've paid for your latest online shopping obsession or split the bill with your buddies. It's like having a personal genie that grants all your financial wishes.

Digital payments come in various forms. You've got mobile wallets, like those apps on your phone that store your card details and let you pay with a simple scan or tap. Then there are online payment platforms that make buying stuff on the internet a breeze, from snazzy clothes to quirky gadgets. And let's not forget about those contactless payments with nifty cards that magically communicate with the payment terminal. Just a case of swishing your card or phone and making your purchase appear like magic.

So, whether you're rocking old-school cash, flaunting your card like a superstar, or dancing through digital payments like a tech-savvy genius, remember that money is the lifeblood of our economic adventures. It's the grease on the wheels of commerce and the ticket to all the fabulous things life has to offer. But be wise and always **spend within your means**, because, as they say, if you look after the pennies the pounds will look after themselves!

Income, expenses, assets, and liabilities.

Alright, buckle up amigos as we're about to embark on a linguistic journey through the land of finance. First stop: Income! Picture income as the money that waltzes its way into your life. It's like that surprise birthday gift from Aunt Mildred that makes your pockets jingle with joy. **Income** can come from various sources, like your job, where you trade your time and skills for a paycheque, or even that lemonade stand you run during the scorching summer holidays when you were a kid. Cha-ching

Now, let's chat about **expenses**, the sneaky ninjas that quietly snatch away your hard-earned cash. Expenses are those little gremlins that hide in the shadows, waiting for the perfect moment to pounce on your wallet. They can be anything from your daily coffee fix to your Netflix subscription, or even that irresistible pair of trainers you just *have to have*. It's important to keep an eye on your expenses and make sure they don't turn into a full-blown Godzilla that tramples over your financial goals.

Next up are **assets**! Assets are like the VIPs of your financial life. They're the fancy things **you own** that can add value and make you feel like a money mogul. Think of your car, your home, or even that vintage comic book collection gathering dust in your attic. Assets have the power to *appreciate in value* over time, like a fine wine that becomes more valuable with age. Just remember, that not all assets are created equal, so choose wisely if you want your wealth to grow.

On the flip side, we have **liabilities**, the mischievous troublemakers that can mess with your financial mojo. Liabilities are those unexpected guests who crash your party and leave you with a huge mess to clean up. They're the **debts and obligations** that drain your financial resources, like that student loan you're still paying off or that credit card balance that keeps growing like irritating weeds. Keep those liabilities in check so they don't throw a wrench in your financial plans.

It's worth noting that not all expenses and liabilities are created equal. Some are like that mandatory broccoli on your dinner plate - necessary for your financial health. These are your essential expenses, like food, shelter, and, of course, a secret stash of chocolate for emergencies. And then there are the non-essential expenses, the tempting treats that can drain your funds faster than you can say "shopaholic." **Balancing** your essential and non-essential expenses is the key to financial well-being and avoiding a broccoli-induced meltdown.

Armed with your newfound knowledge of financial terminology, you're ready to conquer the world of money. Remember, income is your ticket to financial freedom, expenses can be stealthy villains, assets are your rockstar allies, and liabilities are the tricky foes you must conquer. By mastering these terms and finding the right balance, you'll be on your way to financial success.

Expenses and budgets

Budgeting means being the owner of your money kingdom. You get to don your majestic crown, sit on your financial throne, and make all the money decisions. It's being the ruler of your own financial universe, where every pound has a purpose. Just remember, being a budgeting monarch doesn't mean you have to give up all the fun stuff. It's all about finding that sweet spot between saving and splurging.

So, what's a budget? Think of it as a recipe that helps you turn your money into financial bliss. A budget is like a blueprint for your spending, where you assign your ££ to different categories. It's like dividing your allowance into slices of pizza, knowing exactly how many slices you can devour without ending up with an empty plate (aka wallet).

Tracking **expenses**, on the other hand, is the detective on a mission. You whip out your magnifying glass (or smartphone) and go on a hunt to uncover where your money goes. It's following a trail of breadcrumbs, except the breadcrumbs are receipts, online statements, and that suspiciously large pile of takeaway boxes in the bin. Tracking expenses is like shining a spotlight on your spending habits and saying, "Aha! So that's where all my money disappears!"

Let's dive into some real-life examples. Imagine you have a deep, undying love for fancy coffee. You track your expenses and realise you're spending a small fortune at the local coffee shop. Now, armed with this knowledge, you can create a budget category called "Caffeine Adventures" and allocate a certain amount each month to fuel your java cravings. You can even unleash your inner barista and make your own gourmet coffee at home to save some extra dough.

Another example is the ever-elusive dining-out extravaganza. You track your expenses and discover that your weekly Taco Tuesdays and Fish Fridays are gobbling up a significant portion of your budget. Fear not! You can create a budget category called *"Foodie Fun"* and plan to eat out only on special occasions. You might even discover the joy of home-cooked meals and impress your friends with your secret recipe for mouth-watering spag bol.

Let's not forget the world of online shopping, where the temptation to buy random stuff is just a click away. By tracking your expenses, you might uncover a shocking truth: you've been ordering unicorn-shaped slippers and pineapple-shaped watermelons more often than you care to admit. It's time to create a budget category called *"Quirky Collectibles"* and set a monthly spending limit to satisfy your whimsical desires without turning your bank account into a virtual zoo.

Ah, the thrill of entertainment! Tracking your expenses might reveal that you've been going to every concert, movie premiere, and circus performance in town. Now, you can channel your inner event planner and create a budget category called "Epic Entertainment" to allocate funds specifically for those once-in-a-lifetime experiences.

Budgeting and tracking expenses are the dynamic duo of financial superpowers. They give you control over your money kingdom, help you uncover spending habits, and allow you to make informed decisions about where to allocate your precious pounds. Just remember, it's okay to have a little fun along the way. So go forth and conquer your finances.

Chapter 3: Managing Your Money Wisely

The Purpose and Benefits of Budgeting

Let's dive deeper into the world of budgeting, where pounds and pence come together to create financial magic. In this chapter, we'll unravel the mystery behind budgeting and discover why it's the essential skill you need in your financial arsenal. Tune in, and let's embark on this confident and fun journey!

With a budget, you become the master of your **financial destiny**, banish financial stress and bring forth *piece of mind*! It **helps you avoid living pay-cheque to pay-cheque** and frees you from the anxiety of not knowing if you'll have enough to cover your bills. With a budget, you can allocate funds for emergencies, unexpected expenses, or that much-deserved dream holiday. You'll sleep soundly, knowing your financial house is in order. Budgeting is not just about tracking expenses and saving a few bucks here and there; it's about creating a solid foundation for your future. By crafting a budget, you gain a clear understanding of your financial health. You can see where your money is flowing and spot any leaks that may be draining your wallet. This awareness empowers you to make informed decisions about your spending, saving, and investing. Budgeting gives you control over your money, transforming you into that financial trooper!

Budgeting also opens doors to the land of dreams and aspirations. It paves the way for achieving your financial goals, whether it's buying a car, starting a business, or saving for Uni. By wisely managing your money, you're building a strong financial foundation that will support your dreams and make them a reality.

Last but not least, budgeting can be surprisingly fun. Yes, you read that right. It's like a puzzle game where you get to find creative ways to maximise your resources and make your money go further. You can challenge yourself to trim unnecessary expenses or find clever ways to increase your income. Budgeting doesn't have to be a dull spreadsheet affair; it can be an adventure where you uncover hidden treasures within your financial landscape.

Creating a Budget: A Step-by-Step Guide; from clueless to confident

Step 1: Gather Your Financial Tools

First things first, gather your financial arsenal. Grab a pen and paper, fire up a budgeting app on your phone, or get cosy with a trusty spreadsheet on your computer. Choose the tools that work best for you.

Step 2: Track Your Income

Now it's time to unleash the power of numbers! Grab a hold of your recent bank statements, pay stubs, or any other sources of income. Jot down all the cash that flows into your life. Whether it's your pay-cheque, allowance, or that summer job, make sure to include every pound that comes your way.

Step 3: Tame the Beast: Expenses

Time to wrangle those expenses and show them who's boss! Track your spending for the past month or two. Categorise your expenses into groups like groceries, transportation, entertainment, and the occasional unicorn trinket. Be thorough, but don't forget to leave room for those spontaneous ice cream cravings.

Step 4: Set Your Goals

Picture your future self and think about what you want to achieve. Is it a trip around the world? College tuition? Or maybe saving up for that new useless hoverboard? Set your financial goals and write them down. Make them specific, measurable, and sprinkle them with a dash of excitement. Goals are the fuel that powers your budgeting journey.

Step 5: Allocate and Adjust.

Here comes the fun part! Distribute your income among your expenses and goals. Ensure that you have enough allocated for necessities like food, housing, and bills. As you divvy up your funds, don't forget to save for emergencies and *invest in your dreams*. Keep adjusting until the numbers align with your priorities.

Step 6: Stay Committed and Review.

You've created your budgeting masterpiece, but the journey doesn't end here. Stay **committed** to your financial goals and regularly review your budget. Celebrate your victories and make tweaks along the way. Life is like a rollercoaster, and your budget will help you ride it smoothly, even through those unexpected twists and turns.

Budgeting is not just about crunching numbers, it's about taking control of your financial destiny, having fun, and making your money work for you. Unleash your creativity and let the magic begin.

Tips for Managing Expenses, Setting Priorities, and Avoid Overspending

Now that you've embarked on your budgeting journey, it's time to master the art of managing expenses, setting priorities, and dodging the overspending trap.

Tip 1: Get Creative with Your Expenses:

For example, why not host a film night at home with friends instead of splurging on expensive cinema tickets? Or how about swapping clothes with your fashionable buddies to freshen up your wardrobe without breaking the bank? By thinking outside the box, you'll find that saving money can actually be exciting and rewarding!

Tip 2: Set Priorities and Stick to Them:

Envisage you're in town, and everything looks deliciously tempting. But wait! You've got a limited budget, and it's time to set priorities. Identify what truly matters to you and allocate your funds accordingly. Whether it's saving up for a dream holiday, investing in your education, or building an emergency fund, make those priorities the star of your budget. Stay focused and resist the urge to splurge on fleeting desires. Remember, every pound you save brings you closer to your bigger, brighter goals.

Tip 3: Be a Smart Shopper.

Ah, the thrill of the shopping hunt! But beware of the overspending trap lurking around every corner. Before you whip out your wallet, pause and ask yourself, "Do I really need this?" Give yourself a cooling-off period to differentiate between wants and needs. And when you do shop, be a savvy shopper. Compare prices, clip coupons, and take advantage of sales and discounts. Remember, saving money on one shopping spree will allow you to reallocate this windfall elsewhere.

Tip 4: Embrace the Power of Delayed Gratification.

Patience is your secret weapon against overspending. Instead of succumbing to impulsive purchases, practice the art of delayed gratification. When you come across something you desire, take a step back and give it some thought. Sleep on it, and if you still feel the same way after a few days, consider making the purchase. You'll be surprised at how many unnecessary expenses you can dodge by simply allowing yourself some time to reflect.

Tip 5: Find Joy in the Journey.

Budgeting is not just about restricting yourself; it's about finding joy in the journey towards financial freedom. Celebrate every milestone and small victory along the way. Treat yourself to a little reward when you reach a savings goal or stick to your budget for the month. Budgeting is a marathon, not a sprint, and finding pleasure in the process will keep you motivated and committed to your financial success.

Armed with these tips, you're ready to conquer the world of managing expenses, setting priorities, and avoiding the overspending pitfall. Have fun, stay confident, and remember that financial savvy is within reach.

Chapter 4: Saving Strategies for a Brighter Future

What's the point in saving anyway...

It's time to talk about something seriously important: saving money. Saving isn't just about stashing away your hard-earned cash; it's a medium that can transform your future. Imagine a world where you have freedom to pursue your dreams, tackle unexpected challenges with ease, and create a safety net when things go wrong (which they will). This could be you, by unleashing the power of **saving**!

Now, I know what you might be thinking: 'But saving sounds boring, and I want to enjoy my money!' Trust me, I get it. But here's the secret: Saving doesn't mean sacrificing all the fun. It's about finding that sweet spot between enjoying the present and *preparing* for the future. Think of saving as your personal treasure chest, ready to unlock a world of possibilities when the time is right.

Saving money gives you a sense of control and independence. It's the security that can save the day when unexpected expenses pop up or seize exciting opportunities that come your way. Plus, the more you save, the more you'll see your money grow. Watching your savings grow will give you the desire and momentum to continue to save more.

Money Matters Sorted

Let's not forget the peace of mind that saving money brings. Visualise lying on a hammock, sipping a fruity drink, and basking in the sun, knowing that you have a safety net to catch you if life throws a googly (cricketing term). It's the kind of peace that comes from knowing you're prepared and financially resilient. Saving money is the invisible armour that shields you from unexpected financial storms.

And here's the cherry on top: Saving money gives you the **freedom** to pursue your dreams. Want to travel the world? Start a business? Make a difference in your community? Saving is the fuel that powers those dreams. It's like having your own personal genie granting you the financial wishes you've always dreamed of. So let your imagination run wild, and let your savings make those dreams a reality.

In a nutshell, saving money isn't just about stacking coins and notes in a piggy bank. It's about unlocking a world of opportunities, gaining control of your financial destiny, and building a bridge to a brighter future. Later on, I will show you some saving strategies, where you'll discover tips, tricks, and magical ways to make your money grow. Start saving *small amounts* now.

Accounts are not created equal

Let's discuss the wonderful world of savings accounts, where your money can grow and flourish like never before. When it comes to saving for a brighter future, not all accounts are created equal. To start, you will need a current account. This is for day-to-day living, and any surplus money that you have in here could be automated into a savings account.

First up, we have the classic savings account. Think of it as the foundation of your financial fortress. With a traditional savings account, you'll enjoy the peace of mind that comes with knowing your money is safe and easily accessible. It's the perfect option for those who value simplicity and want to start building their savings with ease.

Next, we have the high-yield savings account for maximising your savings potential. These accounts often offer higher interest rates, which means your money grows at a faster pace. You can also lock away your savings for an agreed timeframe, e.g., 12 months. In return, you'll enjoy higher interest rates compared to traditional savings accounts. It's a great choice for those who have a specific savings goal in mind and can afford to let their money grow steadily over time. It's like having a turbocharger strapped to your savings. If you're looking to make every pound count and watch your savings climb that little bit faster, a high-yield savings account could be your go-to choice.

If you're dreaming of a future filled with sun-soaked beaches and leisurely retirement days, a Retirement Account might be just the ticket. These offer tax advantages and allow you to save specifically for later in life. This option may seem for 'older people', as retirement is ages away, but keep in mind the power of **compound growth** (discussed in detail in Chapter 7). Start saving in your late teens or early twenties, and you will be streets ahead of your contemporaries when discussing the merits of early retirement.

For those looking to save for specific purposes like buying a home or funding higher education, specialised savings accounts can be a game-changer. An Individual Savings Account (ISA) might be just the ticket. ISAs offer tax 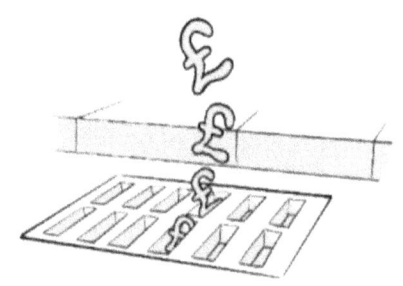 advantages and provide a focused approach to saving for your specific goals. Whether you choose a Cash ISA or an Investment ISA, you'll be taking proactive steps towards your goals in a tax-efficient manner, remembering that tax is one of the greatest **drains** on wealth.

Choosing the right savings account is like finding the perfect fit for your favourite pair of shoes. It's all about considering your financial goals, timelines, and personal preferences. So, take a moment to explore the different types of savings accounts available and find the one that aligns with your aspirations and get ready to watch your savings blossom.

Practical tips for saving

Ready to take your savings game to the next level? Here are some practical tips and strategies that will transform you into a savings superstar. Saving effectively is all about making smart choices and developing good habits that stick. So, fasten your seatbelt as we embark on this exciting savings journey!

Tip #1: Automate your savings.

Set up automatic transfers from your current account to your savings account on a regular basis. Treat it like a monthly subscription to your future self.

Tip #2: Cut back on unnecessary expenses.

Take a closer look at your spending habits and identify areas where you can trim the fat. Let's say you spend £4 on a fancy coffee every day. By brewing your own coffee at home and saving that £4, you could end up with over £1,400 in a year. That's a serious boost to your savings.

Tip #3: Set savings goals.

Having a clear target in mind can be a powerful motivator. Whether it's saving for a dream holiday, a new gadget, or an emergency fund, set specific savings goals and track your progress.

Tip #4: Create a spending plan.

Budgeting doesn't have to be a buzzkill—it's actually your best friend when it comes to saving. Take control of your money by tracking your income and expenses. Identify areas where you can make adjustments and allocate more funds towards your savings.

Tip #5: Make saving a team effort.

Get your family and friends on board with your savings journey. Share your goals and encourage them to join in. You can even challenge each other to save a specific amount within a certain timeframe.

Tip #6: Track your progress.

Keep tabs on how much you're saving and celebrate your milestones along the way. Use apps, spreadsheets, or good old-fashioned pen and paper to monitor your progress. Remember, every pound saved brings you one step closer to financial freedom.

Chapter 5: The Power of Smart Spending

I want that and that and that and...

Ah, the age-old battle between needs and wants—it's time to conquer this financial frontier. Understanding the difference between these two can be a game-changer when it comes to smart spending. So, let's dive in and equip ourselves with the superpower of **discernment**. Get ready to become a savvy spender!

First things first, let's define the terms. Needs are the essential things necessary for our survival and well-being. They include items like food, shelter, clothing, and transport. Wants, on the other hand, are the things we desire that aren't necessary for our basic needs. They are the shiny temptations that make our hearts flutter but aren't crucial for our day-to-day existence.

Is it easy to master the art of prioritisation? When faced with a spending decision, ask yourself, 'Is this item fulfilling a need or a want?' You will need to channel your inner strength and unleash your power of discernment. Another tip to differentiate needs from wants is to consider the long-term impact. Needs tend to have a lasting effect on our well-being and happiness, while wants provide temporary enjoyment. For example, saving up for a reliable car that will safely transport you to school or work fulfils a long-term need, while splurging on the latest high-spec car, and repeating the purchase at the same time every year might bring short-term pleasure but isn't a necessity.

Let's not forget the power of contentment. Recognise that our wants can be influenced by external factors like advertisements and peer pressure. By **cultivating contentment** and appreciating what we already have, we can avoid falling into the trap of unnecessary wants. Embrace the mantra 'I have enough,' and watch your spending choices become more intentional and fulfilling.

Remember, there's nothing wrong with treating yourself to something you want occasionally. It's all about finding a balance. Allocate a portion of your budget for wants, but prioritise your needs first. By doing so, you'll ensure your financial foundation is strong and stable, allowing you to indulge in your wants without compromising your financial well-being.

And finally, remember that the power of smart spending lies in making informed decisions. Before making a purchase, consider its value, quality, and long-term impact on your financial goals. Ask yourself if it aligns with your aims and if there are more cost-effective alternatives available. This way, *you'll* become a savvy spender, and *your* way to becoming financially savvy is to make choices that support *your* well-being.

I want to buy that one...and I want it NOW

By mastering the art of informed decision-making, you can stretch your hard-earned money and make purchases that align with your goals. Get ready to unleash your inner financial detective!

First and foremost, research is your greatest ally. Before making a significant purchase, invest time in gathering information. Read product reviews, compare prices across different retailers, and explore alternatives.

Another crucial aspect is understanding value for money. Consider the quality, durability, and functionality of a product. Evaluate its long-term benefits and potential cost savings. As the saying goes 'for half the price, you'll have to buy it twice'.

Don't underestimate the power of **patience**. Avoid impulsive purchases by taking time to weigh your options. Create a cooling-off period for yourself—wait a day or two before finalising a buying decision. This way, you'll avoid succumbing to short-lived impulses. A timely example of this was when my 10-year-old son had £80 in birthday money burning a hole in his pocket for months. He didn't necessarily need anything, since kids have 'everything' nowadays, but since it was his money, he was entitled to spend it as he wished. He waited 5 months before buying the new Cardiff City kit. I take credit for teaching him delayed gratification and this parenting 'win', since it was I who turned him into a die-hard Cardiff City ~~hooligan~~ supporter.

You know who else exhibits delayed gratification? Really rich people. If a millionaire wanted to buy a Rolls Royce, they wouldn't go out and buy the car outright. They would buy a house or two first and then charge rent to the people living there and then with this rental income they would buy the Rolls Royce.

Being a conscious consumer also means considering the environmental and social impact of your purchases. Support companies that align with your values, such as those committed to sustainability or fair-trade practices. Before making a purchase, ask yourself if it aligns with your needs, values, and long-term goals, and separate your desires from genuine needs.

Timing is everything when it comes to finding deals. Keep an eye out for seasonal sales, clearance events, or special promotions. My father-in-law bought me a snow shovel in the summer since it was only 50p. In 10 years, I have used it twice to shovel snow, but it is invaluable for picking up leaves during the autumn months. Retailers often offer significant discounts during holidays or end-of-season sales. Plan your purchases accordingly, and you'll maximise your savings.

Comparison shopping is a skill you must hone. Don't settle for the first option that catches your eye. Instead, explore different retailers, both online and offline, to find the best deal. Use price comparison websites, apps, and even visit a shop like in the olden days to ensure you're getting the most bang for your buck. Take it one step further by harnessing the power of loyalty programmes and discount codes. Sign up for these loyalty programmes at your favourite shops to access exclusive discounts and rewards. Additionally, before completing an online purchase, search for discount codes or coupons that may be applicable.

Last but not least, trust your **instincts**. Sometimes, despite all the research and advice, you'll have a gut feeling about a purchase. If something doesn't feel right, listen to that inner voice.

Chapter 6: Credit and Debt: Making Informed Choices

Give me SOME credit...

Let's talk about credit, the cool concept that lets you buy stuff now and pay for it later. Basically, when you use credit, you're **borrowing** money with the promise to pay it back in the future. It's like getting a mini-loan to fund your shopping spree or that concert ticket you've been eyeing.

Credit scores are like your financial report card; they show how responsible you are with money. Think of it as a number that rates your money skills. The higher the number, the better you're doing! It's calculated based on things like paying your bills on time, how much money you owe, and how long you've been using credit. So, to gain a high credit score, pay your bills on time and avoid racking up too much debt.

Your credit report is like a secret file that has all the juicy details about your financial history. It shows things like your credit accounts, how much money you owe, and even if you've ever had any financial hiccups. It's important to keep an eye on this report because it affects your credit score and how lenders view you.

There are credit agencies that gather all the info for your credit report. They're like the crusaders of credit information, Experian for example. It's a good idea to occasionally check your credit score particularly if you are looking to borrow a considerable sum of money e.g., for a mortgage. A higher credit score generally indicates a lower risk to lenders and in some cases can help you secure better loan terms and interest rates.

Start by making timely payments on your bills and keeping your credit card balances low. It's like defeating those money monsters that might drag your credit score down. Also, having a mix of different types of credit, like a credit card or a small loan, shows that you can handle different financial challenges.

Understanding credit, credit scores, and reports is like mastering a new dance move. It may seem tricky at first, but with practice and a little bit of financial knowledge, you'll be grooving through the world of credit and debt like a pro. So, remember to be **responsible**, pay your bills on time, and keep your credit in check. It's important to use credit wisely, only borrow what you can afford to repay, and make timely payments to maintain a healthy financial future. By doing that, you'll unlock a whole world of financial opportunities.

I am RESPONSIBLE

Let's dive into the wild world of credit cards and talk about how to use them responsibly. Credit cards can be powerful tools that grant you the ability to buy things with a simple swipe or tap. They provide convenience, build your credit history, and offer protection for your purchases. But remember, with great power comes great responsibility!

When it comes to credit cards, think of them as your trusty sidekick, always there to save the day when you need a little financial boost. But just like any sidekick, they can turn into supervillains if you're not careful. That's why it's essential to use your credit card wisely and avoid getting trapped in the clutches of debt. **Always** pay your bills on time. If you forget and make a late payment, you will be charged high interest and may damage your credit score. It is imperative that **automatic** payments are set up from your current account to pay off your credit card to avoid this situation.

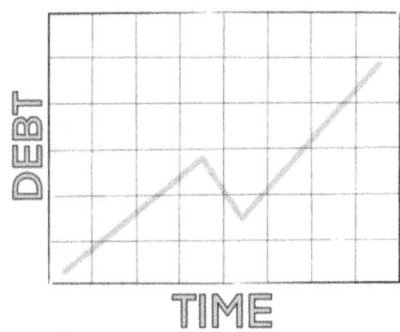

It's tempting to use a credit card for every little purchase, but it's important to be *selective*. Use it for planned expenses or emergencies, like that unicorn-themed concert you've been dreaming about or fixing your jet-powered roller skates.

One of the sneaky villains lurking around credit cards is interest. It's like a mischievous creature that charges you extra money if you don't pay your full balance each month. So, to keep that interest beast at bay, make sure to pay your credit card bill on time and in full. That way, you won't have to worry about it gobbling up your hard-earned cash.

Another danger to watch out for is the Debt Monster. It's like a shadowy creature that grows bigger and scarier the more you owe. To keep this monster in check, only charge what you can afford to pay back. Remember, a credit card is not free money—

it's more like a delayed payment spell. So, be **mindful** of your spending and keep the Debt Monster from haunting your dreams.

Being a credit card superhero means being responsible and staying on top of your finances. Keep track of your spending, set a budget, and regularly check your credit card statements for any unexpected surprises. By staying vigilant and using your credit card wisely, you'll not only protect yourself from financial villains but also build a strong credit history, setting you up for a bright and financially empowered future.

Arrrggghhhhh I'm in debt

Understanding how to manage and pay off debt is a crucial skill for a successful future. Here are some practical guidance on managing and paying off debt effectively, empowering you to make informed choices and build a strong financial foundation.

Assess Your Debt:

Start by taking stock of your debts. Make a list of each debt, including the amount owed, interest rate, minimum monthly payment, and due dates. This overview will help you understand the scope of your debt and prioritise your repayment strategy.

Create a Budget:

Budgeting is a powerful tool for managing and paying off debt. Track your income and expenses to see where your money is going. Identify areas where you can cut back on unnecessary expenses and allocate more funds towards debt repayment. By creating a budget, you'll gain better control over your finances.

Prioritise High-Interest Debt:

Focus on paying off high-interest debt first. These are the debts with the highest interest rates, such as credit card balances or payday loans. By tackling these debts aggressively, you'll reduce the overall interest you'll pay and free up more money for other financial goals.

Cut Expenses and Increase Income:

Look for ways to reduce your expenses and increase your income. Cut back on non-essential spending, such as eating out or buying expensive gadgets. Consider taking on part-time work or freelancing to earn extra money. By making these adjustments, you'll have more funds available for debt repayment.

Use the Snowball or Avalanche Method:

There are two popular strategies for debt repayment. With the snowball method, you start by paying off the smallest debt first while making minimum payments on other debts. Once that debt is cleared, you move on to the next smallest one. This method provides motivation as you see quick wins. The avalanche method focuses on paying off debts with the highest interest rates first, saving you more money in the long run. Choose the method that suits your preferences and financial situation.

Seek Support and Guidance:

Dealing with debt can be overwhelming, but you don't have to go through it alone. Seek support from family, friends, or online communities that can provide encouragement and share their experiences. Additionally, consider reaching out to a financial adviser or credit counsellor for professional guidance tailored to your specific circumstances.

Avoid Accumulating New Debt:

As you work towards paying off existing debt, it's crucial to avoid accumulating new debt. Be mindful of your spending habits and distinguish between wants and needs. Pause before making impulsive purchases and think about whether they align with your financial goals. Developing disciplined spending habits will help you break the cycle of debt and stay on track.

Managing and paying off debt effectively requires discipline and determination, but the rewards are worth it. By assessing your debt, creating a budget, prioritising high-interest debts, and seeking support, you'll be well on your way. Remember, it's a journey, and progress may take time. Stay committed, be patient, and celebrate each milestone along the way. With **persistence**, you'll not only become debt-free but also develop invaluable financial skills that will set you up for a successful and secure future.

Money Matters Sorted

Chapter 7: Exploring the World of Investments

I wish they taught me this in school

Welcome to the exciting world of investments. Here, we'll dive into the concept of investing and explore its possible benefits. Understanding investing at a young age can set you on a path to financial success and provide opportunities for your future. It offers a range of potential benefits, including the opportunity to grow your wealth, beat inflation, and achieve long-term financial goals. One of the most powerful forces that work in favour of young investors is the magic of compound interest.

"Compound interest is the eighth wonder of the world. He who understands it earns it ... he who doesn't ... pays it."

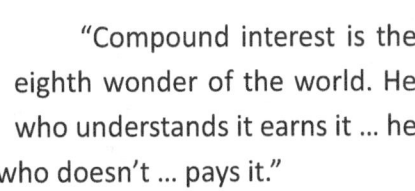

Albert Einstein

Here's an example. If you were to be given a sum of money in 30 days, which option would you choose?
- a) £10 million in one go
- b) A £1 coin will be given to you now, and its amount will double every day for the coming 30 days, i.e., it will become £2 tomorrow, £4 the day after tomorrow, £8 two days after tomorrow, and so on.

Most people would go for the £10 million option, as it is hard to imagine that £1 doubling 30 times will become £1.07 billion! This is the power of compounding.

What is Investing?

Investing is the practice of using your money to purchase assets with the expectation of generating a profit or increasing their value over time. Instead of simply saving your money, investing allows you to put it to work and potentially grow it over the long term. Investments come in various forms, such as stocks, bonds, unit trusts, property, and more. Investing needs to become a habit that you will endure throughout your working life.

Growing your money:

One of the key benefits of investing is the potential to build wealth.

By investing wisely, you give your money the opportunity to grow. Over time, this compounding effect can lead to significant growth, allowing you to achieve financial goals such as buying a home, starting a business, funding your education or retiring early.

Beat Inflation:

Inflation refers to the gradual increase in the cost of goods and services over time. By investing, you give your money the chance to grow at a rate that keeps pace with or even outpaces inflation. This means your purchasing power won't erode over the long term, and your money will retain its value.

Diversification:

Investing allows you to diversify your portfolio, which means spreading your investments across different asset classes and industries. Diversification helps reduce the risk of losing all your money if one investment performs poorly. By diversifying, you can potentially maximise returns while minimising the impact of any single investment's performance.

Funding your dreams:

Investing can provide a pathway to financial independence. As your investments grow, you may reach a point where your returns outpace your expenses, allowing you to rely on your investments for income. This financial independence gives you more control over your life choices, giving you the freedom to pursue your passions and live life on your terms.

Learning Financial Skills:

Engaging in investing at a young age is an excellent opportunity to develop important financial skills. Investing teaches you about financial markets, risk management, and the power of patience and long-term thinking. These skills will serve you well throughout your life, helping you make informed financial decisions and navigate the ever-changing landscape of the economy.

Investing is an exciting and powerful tool that can shape your financial future. By understanding the concept of investing and its potential benefits, you're taking a proactive step towards building wealth and achieving your goals. Remember, investing involves risks, and it's important to educate yourself, seek advice when needed, and start with a clear investment plan. So, embrace the world of investments, be patient, and enjoy the journey of growing your money for a brighter and more prosperous future.

Stocks and Shares, Shares and Stocks

Here, we'll explore different investment options that can help you grow your money and achieve your financial goals. Understanding these options will give you the knowledge and confidence to make informed investment decisions. So, let's dive into the exciting realm of stocks, bonds, and unit trusts!

Stocks (and Shares):

Stocks are like owning a small piece of a company. When you buy stocks, you become a shareholder, sharing in the company's success and growth. The value of stocks can fluctuate based on various factors like market conditions, company performance, and investor sentiment. Investing in stocks can be thrilling and rewarding, but it's important to do your research and consider your risk tolerance before jumping in. A diversified portfolio of stocks will include upward of 30 different companies.

Bonds (and Gilts):

Bonds are like loans you provide to companies (or governments). When you invest in bonds, you become a lender, and the issuer pays you interest over time. Bonds are generally considered safer than stocks because they offer fixed income and have lower volatility. They can be a good option for those seeking more stability in their investment portfolio. However, it's important to assess the creditworthiness of the issuer and understand the risks involved.

Unit Trusts:

Unit trusts, also known as mutual funds or collective investment schemes, pool money from multiple investors to invest in a diversified portfolio of assets. This can include stocks and bonds. A convenient way for small investors to access a professionally managed, diversified investment portfolio is through Unit Trusts. It allows you to invest in a variety of assets with a smaller initial investment. However, do your due diligence and understand the fees and charges associated with unit trusts before investing.

Exchange-Traded Funds (ETFs):

ETFs are investment funds traded on stock exchanges, similar to stocks. They offer the benefit of diversification by tracking a specific index or a basket of assets. ETFs can be a cost-effective way to gain exposure to various asset classes, including stocks, bonds, and commodities. They provide flexibility and liquidity as they can be bought and sold throughout the trading day.

Real Estate Investment Trusts (REITs):
REITs are investment vehicles that allow individuals to invest in real estate without directly owning properties. They own, operate, or finance income-generating properties like office buildings, shopping centres, or apartments. Investing in REITs can provide exposure to the real estate market (commercial property) and potential income through rentals and dividends. However, it's important to consider factors like property market conditions and management quality before investing in REITs.

When exploring different investment options, it's important to consider your risk appetite. Stocks and unit trusts, for example, can offer higher potential returns but also come with higher risks. Bonds and REITs, on the other hand, are generally considered lower risk investment but may offer more modest returns. Diversification across different asset classes can help manage risk by spreading your investments and reducing exposure to any single investment.

By understanding different investment options, you have a wider range of choices to grow your wealth. Each option comes with its own benefits and risks, so it's essential to consider your financial goals, risk tolerance, and do thorough **research** before making investment decisions. Remember, investing is a journey, and as a young adult, you have time on your side. Start small, diversify your portfolio, and always continue learning to make the most of your investments for a financially secure future.

Daniel Jones

A bit of risk is OK....is it?

Investing is not just about making money—it's about managing risks and growing your ~~dosh~~ money over time. So, let's dive into the world of risk management and discover effective strategies for long-term investment success.

Before investing your hard-earned money, it's crucial to understand risk. Risk refers to the potential for investment values to fluctuate, leading to gains or losses. Different investments carry different levels of risk. Stocks, for example, tend to be more volatile than bonds. By understanding and assessing the risks associated with different investments, you'll be better prepared to make informed decisions.

Diversification is a powerful risk management tool. It involves spreading your investments across different asset classes, such as stocks, bonds, and other investment vehicles. By diversifying, you reduce the impact of any single investment's performance on your overall portfolio.

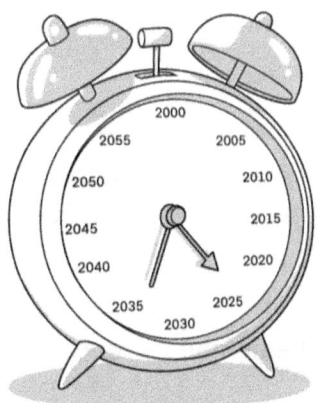

Investing is a **long-term** game. By starting early and giving your investments time to grow, you can benefit from the snowballing effect of compounding. The longer you invest, the more your money can potentially grow. Don't take my word for it, listen to Albert Einstein.

During volatile market conditions in particular, pound-cost averaging is your best friend (particularly for inexperienced investors). It is a strategy that involves investing a fixed amount of money at regular intervals, regardless of market conditions. By contributing the same amount consistently, you buy investments when prices are low as well as when they are priced higher. This strategy helps smooth out the impact of market volatility and can be a great way to build wealth over time.

Investing can be exciting, but it's important to keep emotions in check. Market fluctuations and short-term volatility are a part of investing. Avoid making impulsive decisions based on fear or greed. Instead, focus on your long-term goals and stick to your investment plan. Remember, successful investing requires discipline and a steady hand.

> While you can learn a lot on your own, seeking professional advice is a wise move, especially as you navigate complex investment strategies. Financial advisers can provide guidance based on your individual goals, risk tolerance, and financial situation. They can help you design an investment plan that aligns with your long-term objectives and guide you through different market conditions.

The investment landscape is constantly evolving, so if you have the confidence to invest yourself, stay informed by following financial news, reading books, and attending seminars or workshops. The more you learn, the better equipped you'll be to make informed investment decisions. Remember, knowledge is power!

Managing risk and implementing long-term investment strategies are essential for your financial success. By understanding risk, diversifying your portfolio, embracing the power of time, practicing pound-cost averaging, and keeping emotions in check, you'll be on the path to long-term wealth accumulation. Seek professional advice when needed, continue learning, and adapt your investment strategy as you grow. Investing is a journey, so buckle up, stay focused, and enjoy the bumpy ride to financial prosperity!

Pensions are for old people

Well, they are for older people, but the accumulation or saving phase is conducted when people are young. **The younger, the better.** Tune in, this is important: let's unleash the power of tax relief and explore how it can supercharge your investments.

Tax relief is where the UK government will give you an extra 25% on your pension contribution, effectively giving you more money to invest (if earning the average salary in the UK). For example, if you're a basic rate taxpayer and contribute £100 to your pension, the government adds an additional £25 as tax-relief. That's like getting free money to supercharge your savings! There is genuine concern in the UK that the population is not saving enough for later in life, so the government will give a simple 'tax-break' for those who do.

As you contribute to your pension over time, these tax-relief contributions will compound, growing alongside your investments. The downside: This money will be stored away until you're in your late 50s. If this is OK with you, then by investing in this tax-efficient manner, you're not only taking advantage of the power of compound growth but also leveraging tax relief to make your hard-earned money work harder for you.

Here is an example that could be followed: Saving £80 per week from age 20 as cash (i.e., no interest gained) will leave you with £160,000 at age 60, if you can't afford £80 ask your parents or grandparents to contribute £40 towards your future whilst you stump-up the other £40. If that £80 is invested for your retirement (claiming government tax relief) and invested at 5% growth, your final pot could be £677,000 at age 60, and if invested at 8% growth, it will leave you with £1,440,000. Of course, there are no guarantees with investing, so these final figures could be more or less than those stated, but at least you will give your money the **opportunity** to grow over these 40 years.

Chapter 8: Navigating the Job Market: Career and Income

Everyday is a school day...

Welcome to the world of careers and income! This chapter is all about helping you navigate the job market with confidence and a dash of humour. Fasten your seat belt and get ready to explore the importance of education, skills, and career choices—a trio that can unlock the doors to a fulfilling and financially rewarding future!

Education, education, education. It's not just about memorising facts and figures; it's about gaining knowledge, critical thinking skills, and a thirst for learning. Remember, education doesn't stop after school—it's a lifelong adventure of growth and discovery. So, embrace your inner knowledge seeker and let education be your PA to an enjoyable career.

Skills are the spices that make you stand out in a crowded job market. Whether it's mastering a programming language, honing your communication skills, or becoming a pro at problem-solving, skills are your secret weapon to landing that dream job. So, spice up your skill set and let your unique flavours shine!

Choosing a career path is like picking your favourite flavour of ice cream—exciting and personal! It's important to **follow your passions and interests**. Don't just chase money; chase fulfilment and joy. Find a career that aligns with your values, allows you to pursue your passions, and brings out the best in you. Remember, a job you love is a recipe for success.

But here's a fun twist—career choices aren't set in stone. It's more like a buffet where you can try different dishes until you find your favourite. So don't be afraid to explore, experiment, and pivot along the way. Sometimes, unexpected choices lead to the most delicious outcomes.

Always sprinkle some humour into your career journey. Embrace failures and setbacks as learning opportunities.

Remember that awkward interview or that not-so-perfect job? They're all part of the recipe that shapes you. So, laugh at the blunders, learn from them, and keep moving forward. After all, life's too short to take yourself too seriously.

While education, skills, and career choices are vital ingredients, it's important to add a pinch of adaptability to the mix. The job market is ever-changing, and being open to new possibilities and flexible in your approach can lead to unexpected adventures and opportunities. Embrace change, embrace growth, and let your career story unfold.

Finally, remember that your career journey is **unique** to you. Don't compare yourself to others or get caught up in societal expectations. It's *your* life, *your* choices, and *your* path to success. Follow your heart, sprinkle in your own flavours, and savour the sweet taste of a career that brings you joy and financial prosperity. This mindset will help you make informed decisions and navigate the job market with confidence and joy.

Time for a job

Welcome to the world of job searching, where opportunities abound and dreams come true! As you embark on this exhilarating journey, equip yourself with the tools to navigate the job market like a seasoned adventurer. Let's dive into the art of job searching, CV building, and interview skills.

First, let's conquer the art of job searching. Approach it like a treasure hunt, seeking out the hidden gems of employment. Harness the power of online job boards, company websites, and professional networking platforms to uncover opportunities that align with your aspirations. Be persistent, resilient, and proactive in your pursuit, and watch as doors of opportunity swing open!

Next, craft a winning CV that showcases your skills and experiences. Think of it as your personal marketing brochure, designed to catch the eye of potential employers. Tailor your CV to highlight your strengths, accomplishments, and relevant qualifications. Remember, **confidence** is key, so let your CV sparkle with pride!

Preparing for interviews is like rehearsing for a captivating performance. Research the company, anticipate common interview questions, and craft thoughtful responses that showcase your expertise. Practice your interviewing skills with a trusted friend or family member, honing your ability to communicate effectively and authentically. You're a star, so shine brightly during your interview.

During the interview, exude confidence and professionalism while letting your true **personality** shine through. Dress the part, maintain good posture, and establish genuine connections with your interviewers. Mention your hobbies such as football or travelling and if the interviewer picks up on these, react and start a genuine conversation. This will instantly relax you and show your true self. Remember, you're not just a job candidate; you're a valuable asset ready to make a difference.

Be prepared to ask thoughtful questions during the interview. This demonstrates your genuine interest in the role and the company. Inquire about the company culture, career growth opportunities, and how your role contributes to the organisation's success. Show them you're not just looking for a job but for a meaningful and fulfilling career.

After the interview, follow up with a thank-you note or email expressing your gratitude for the opportunity to interview. This simple gesture showcases your professionalism and leaves a lasting impression. It's like sprinkling a touch of magic on your candidacy.

And remember, even if you face setbacks, which you will, don't lose heart. Each experience, whether successful or not, offers valuable lessons and growth. Embrace resilience, bouncing back stronger and more determined than ever.

So, there you have it, future job market conquerors! Armed with effective job-search strategies, a polished CV, and stellar interview skills, you're ready to embark on a journey towards career success. With confidence in your abilities and a touch of finesse, you'll navigate the job market with grace and secure the opportunities that align with your dreams. Best of luck on your thrilling career quest!

I want more pay please..

Congratulations! You've landed a job offer—a testament to your skills and potential. Now, it's time to embrace the art of salary negotiation and give your financial growth an early boost. Remember, you deserve to be fairly compensated for your talents and contributions. So, let's dive into the world of negotiation with confidence and finesse.

First and foremost, research is your secret weapon. Understand the industry standards and salary ranges for your position, taking into account factors like experience, qualifications, and location. Armed with this knowledge, you can enter the negotiation phase with confidence, knowing your worth.

During negotiations, approach the conversation with a collaborative mindset. Clearly **articulate** your accomplishments, skills, and the value you bring to the table. Be confident yet respectful in expressing your desired compensation package. Remember, it's a negotiation, and finding a mutually beneficial outcome is the goal.

Keep in mind that salary isn't the only factor to consider. Look at the entire compensation package, including benefits, bonuses, and opportunities for growth and **advancement**. Evaluate these components holistically to ensure they align with your long-term financial goals.

Remember, negotiation is a skill that extends beyond just the initial job offer. As you progress in your career, seize opportunities to negotiate salary increases, promotions, and additional perks. Continually assess and communicate your value to your employer, fostering a culture of ongoing growth and development.

While negotiating, be open to creative solutions that benefit both you and your employer. Consider flexible work arrangements, professional development opportunities, or performance-based incentives. Embrace a win-win mindset, where you can drive your financial growth while contributing to the success of the organisation.

Financial growth goes hand in hand with personal and professional development. Invest in yourself—acquire new skills, pursue advanced education, and seek opportunities for career growth. As you enhance your knowledge and expertise, you become more valuable in the job market, opening doors to higher-paying roles.

Finally, remember that financial growth is not solely about earning a higher salary. It also involves effective budgeting, saving, and investing. Make wise financial decisions, live within your means, and prioritise building a strong financial foundation. By managing your finances wisely, you create a solid platform for long-term financial growth and security.

There you have it, aspiring negotiators and financial growth enthusiasts! With research, confidence, and a collaborative mindset, you can navigate the intricacies of salary negotiation and cultivate your financial growth. Embrace the power of knowing your worth and advocate for fair compensation, while continuously investing in your personal and professional development. As you embark on this journey, may your financial future be filled with abundance and success. Go forth and conquer!

Chapter 9: Entrepreneurship - Turning Ideas into Financial Success

I'm the BOSS

Welcome to the captivating realm of entrepreneurship (being self-employed), where dreams are transformed into reality and possibilities are limitless. Entrepreneurship is the art of creating, launching, and growing a business venture driven by passion, innovation, and a desire to make a difference in the world. It's a thrilling path that offers tremendous **potential** for financial success and personal fulfilment.

At its core, entrepreneurship is about identifying a problem or a need in the market and developing a unique solution. It's about challenging the status quo, embracing risk, and having the courage to pursue your vision. By bringing value to customers, you have the opportunity to build a thriving business and enjoy the rewards that come with it.

One of the most rewarding aspects of entrepreneurship is the ability to take control of your destiny. As an entrepreneur, you have the freedom to chart your own course, make decisions that align with your values, and shape your business according to your vision. This level of autonomy can be incredibly empowering and fulfilling.

Financial success is a significant motivator in the world of entrepreneurship. While it requires hard work, dedication, and perseverance, the rewards can be substantial. As an entrepreneur, you have the potential to generate wealth, create multiple income streams, and achieve financial independence. However, it's important to remember that financial success is not guaranteed and often comes as a result of strategic planning, effective execution, and adaptability.

In addition to financial rewards, entrepreneurship offers a range of intangible benefits. It allows you to pursue your passions, follow your purpose, and make a meaningful impact on society. By building a successful business, you can create job opportunities, contribute to economic growth, and inspire others to chase their dreams.

Entrepreneurship is a journey of continuous learning and growth. It requires a diverse skill set encompassing areas such as leadership, problem-solving, marketing, finance, and innovation. The process of building and running a business provides ample opportunities for personal and professional development, expanding your knowledge and capabilities along the way.

Remember, entrepreneurship is not just about starting a business; it's a mindset—a way of thinking and approaching the world. It's about being resourceful, embracing challenges, and seizing opportunities. Whether you're starting a small venture or dreaming of building an empire, the rewards of entrepreneurship are within reach if you have the passion, determination, and resilience to persevere.

So, if you're ready to embark on an exhilarating journey filled with excitement, challenges, and endless possibilities, entrepreneurship may be the perfect path for you. Embrace your entrepreneurial spirit, nurture your ideas, and let your creativity soar. The potential rewards are waiting to be discovered, and the journey begins now.

With these insights, you can now step confidently into the world of entrepreneurship, armed with knowledge of its potential rewards. Let your passion guide you, and may your entrepreneurial journey be filled with success, fulfilment, and the satisfaction of turning your ideas into a thriving business.

I'm going to be a millionaire: 7 steps to get there

1. The Spark of Brilliance:

So, you've got an idea that's just itching to be turned into a flourishing business? That's fantastic! The first step in this

exhilarating journey is to let your creativity run wild. Brainstorm ideas, scribble them down on napkins, and dream big.

2. From Idea to Action:

Once you've settled on your million-dollar idea (or at least a pretty decent one), it's time to put your plan into action. Start by researching the market, analysing the competition, and determining the demand for your product or service. Get ready to dive into the depths of feasibility studies and financial projections. It may sound daunting but fear not! You're a future business tycoon in the making.

3. The Paperwork Tango:

Ah, paperwork, the dance partner of every budding entrepreneur. Embrace it, my friend. Register your business name, secure the necessary licences and permits, and familiarise yourself with the legal requirements. Don't worry; it's just a few steps of fancy footwork before you can hit the entrepreneurial dance floor!

4. Funding Frenzy:

Money, moolah, dough – call it what you will, you need it to get your business off the ground. Prepare to wear your fundraising hat and explore different financing options. From using your savings to seeking investments or grants, there's a world of financial opportunities waiting for you. Remember, convincing potential investors is like a well-choreographed dance routine – confidence, charisma, and a killer pitch.

5. Assemble Your Dream Team:

Few build a successful business alone. Find people who complement your skills and share your vision. Whether it's a co-founder, employees, or even a mentor, surround yourself with talented individuals who can help you turn your dream into a reality. Together, you'll tango your way to success!

6. Marketing Magic:

Now that you've set the stage, it's time to let the world know about your fabulous new venture. Create a marketing plan, establish your brand identity, and make your presence felt in the digital and physical realms. From social media sorcery to captivating content, your marketing efforts will ensure your business waltzes into the hearts and wallets of your target audience.

7. Launch and Learn:

Drumroll, please! It's time for the grand opening of your entrepreneurial masterpiece. Launch your business, celebrate your hard work, and be prepared to learn as you go. Entrepreneurship is a continuous dance of adaptation and innovation. Embrace the inevitable missteps, pivot when necessary, and always keep your entrepreneurial spirit burning brightly.

Remember that starting a business is an exhilarating journey filled with twirls, dips, and spins. With confidence, perseverance, and a touch of light-heartedness, you're well on your way to turning your entrepreneurial dreams into a reality.

Where to start?

Building a Business Plan:

Ah, the business plan—a roadmap to guide you through the wild, exhilarating world of entrepreneurship. Start by defining your vision, mission, and goals. Consider your target market, analyse the competition, and outline your marketing and sales strategies. Don't forget to add a sprinkle of your unique personality to make it shine! A well-crafted business plan is the secret to success—a pinch of passion, a dash of strategy, and a dollop of **optimism!**

Taming the Financial Beast:

Money—sometimes it feels like the wild stallion of the entrepreneurial journey. But fear not! You can master the art of managing your finances. Keep meticulous records of your income and expenses, create budgets, and track your cash flow. Be frugal, but don't forget to treat yourself once in a while (ice cream does wonders for the soul!). Remember, managing your finances is like walking a tightrope—balance is key.

Creative Juices Unleashed:

Creativity adds flavour and charm to your business. So, let your imagination run wild and embrace the magic of brainstorming sessions! Encourage yourself and your team to think outside the box, explore new ideas, and take calculated risks. Remember, creativity is the colourful confetti cannon—sprinkle it everywhere and watch your business sparkle.

The Customer Connection:

In the realm of entrepreneurship, customers are royalty, and connecting with them is a delightful dance. Understand their needs, listen to their feedback, and provide top-notch customer service. Show them that you genuinely care, and they'll be your biggest cheerleaders. Customer satisfaction is the secret ingredient that turns your business into a love affair. Woo them with your charm, and they'll be loyal for life!

Embrace the Power of Networking:

Ah, networking—the art of building connections and expanding your social circle. Attend industry events, join professional organisations, and connect with like-minded individuals. Strike up

conversations, exchange business cards, and let your passion shine through. Remember, networking is like a friendly game of tag—when you're "it," chase your dreams and make **meaningful connections** along the way!

Fail Forward:

Mistakes—they're like the pesky paparazzi of entrepreneurship, always lurking around. But here's the secret: failure is not the end; it's a steppingstone to success! Embrace your failures, learn from them, and grow stronger. Don't be afraid to take risks and make mistakes—it's all part of the thrilling entrepreneurial journey. Even better is to learn from other people's mistakes. If you see someone with a good idea but you think they are not utilising their idea to

its full potential, there may be an opportunity for you to make a success of it.

Celebrate Victories Big and Small:

Entrepreneurship is a rollercoaster ride with thrilling highs and stomach-churning lows. Amidst the twists and turns, don't forget to celebrate your victories, big and small. Whether it's landing your first client, hitting a sales milestone, or simply conquering a daunting challenge, take a moment to pat yourself on the back.

There you have it, my entrepreneurial friend—tips to develop a stellar business plan, manage your finances, and foster creativity with flair! With confidence and passion, you're well on your way to entrepreneurial greatness. Don't talk about it, just do it!

Chapter 10: Giving Back - Philanthropy and Community Impact

Time to give back

Giving back and making a positive impact is a powerful way to create a ripple effect of change in a tiny bit of the world. It's not just about money; it's about making a difference in the lives of others and the communities we are a part of. When we give back, we contribute to the greater good and help address social issues. Whether it's volunteering our time, donating resources, or using our skills to benefit others, we can make a tangible difference in people's lives.

Philanthropy and community impact teach us important values like **empathy**, compassion, and gratitude. By actively engaging in acts of giving, we develop a greater understanding of the challenges others face and gain a sense of appreciation for what we have. Giving back also provides a sense of fulfilment and purpose. When we see the positive impact we can make, it boosts our self-esteem and overall well-being. We realise that our actions matter and that we have the ability to positively influence the community around us.

Philanthropy is not limited to financial resources. It's about leveraging our skills, knowledge, and networks to support causes we care about. We all have unique talents and strengths that can be utilised to make a difference, whether it's mentoring someone,

organising fundraisers, or advocating for social change. By engaging in philanthropic activities, we become part of something bigger than ourselves. We connect with like-minded individuals, organisations, and communities who are passionate about creating positive change. This sense of belonging and collaboration further amplifies the impact we can have.

Teaching young people about the importance of giving back instils **lifelong values**. When teenagers actively participate in philanthropic activities, they develop a sense of responsibility and become more aware of the needs of others. These experiences shape them into compassionate and socially conscious adults.

Giving back can also be a valuable learning experience. It exposes us to different cultures, perspectives, and challenges. By stepping outside our comfort zones and immersing ourselves in unfamiliar situations, we gain a broader understanding of the world and become more adaptable individuals.

Making a **positive** impact doesn't have to be overwhelming or grandiose. Small acts of kindness and generosity can have a significant effect. Even a smile, a listening ear, or a kind word can brighten someone's day and create a ripple effect of positivity.

Ultimately, giving back and making a positive impact is not only about helping others; it also enriches our own lives. It brings joy, fulfilment, and a sense of purpose. As we strive to build a better future, let's remember that we all have the power to make a difference, and by doing so, we create a world that is worth living in.

Remember, giving back and making a positive impact is an incredible journey that we can embark on at any age. So let's join hands, inspire others, and create a better world together, one act of kindness at a time.

Charity begins... everywhere

Volunteering your time is a wonderful way to get involved in charitable activities. There are countless organisations and causes that rely on volunteers to support their initiatives. Whether it's helping out at a local food bank, assisting in animal shelters, or participating in community clean-up events, volunteering allows you to directly contribute to the betterment of your community.

Organising fundraisers and events is another impactful way to make a difference. You can rally your friends, family, and community members to support a cause you're passionate about. From charity runs and bake sales to art exhibitions and benefit concerts, these events not only raise funds but also create awareness and bring people together for a common cause.

Donating money or resources is a straightforward way to support charitable organisations. You can choose to make regular contributions or give a one-time donation based on your financial capacity. Research reputable nonprofits or causes aligned with your values and goals, ensuring that your resources go where they are needed most. Remember, even small donations can add up and make a meaningful impact.

Using your skills and expertise to benefit others is a unique way to contribute to charitable activities. If you have a particular skill set, such as graphic design, writing, or web development, you can offer your services to nonprofits or community projects in need. Your skills can help these organisations create engaging marketing materials, compelling content, or an online presence, amplifying their reach and impact.

Advocating for social change is an important way to get involved in charitable activities. By raising awareness about pressing issues and actively engaging in conversations, you can help drive positive change. This can involve sharing information on social media, attending community meetings or protests, or writing letters to policymakers. Your voice has the power to influence opinions and policies, shaping a more just and equitable society.

Remember, there is no one-size-fits-all approach to getting involved in charitable activities. Find what resonates with you and aligns with your interests and values. Whether it's volunteering, fundraising, donating, utilising your skills, or advocating for change, each act of kindness and support brings us closer to creating a better world. So, explore the options available, follow your passion, and embark on a fulfilling journey of giving back and making a **positive impact.**

You are doing this for others...and yourself

Volunteering and engaging in philanthropic activities provide numerous personal and financial benefits. On a personal level, volunteering allows you to develop new skills, expand your network, and gain valuable experience. By dedicating your time and energy to a cause you care about, you can enhance your leadership abilities, improve your *communication* skills, and cultivate a sense of empathy and **compassion.**

Volunteering also offers the opportunity to explore new interests and discover hidden talents. Through hands-on involvement in charitable activities, you might find that you have a knack for event planning, public speaking, or project management. These newfound skills can be leveraged in various areas of your life, including your career, leading to personal growth and increased job prospects.

In addition to personal growth, engaging in philanthropy can have a positive impact on your financial well-being. By giving back to your community and supporting causes you believe in, you create a sense of fulfilment and purpose, which can contribute to overall happiness and life satisfaction. Studies have shown that individuals who engage in charitable giving tend to experience greater personal happiness and a sense of abundance.

Volunteering and philanthropy can also have financial benefits in the form of tax deductions. Depending on your country's tax laws, donations to eligible charitable organisations may be tax-deductible. This can provide an opportunity to reduce your taxable income, potentially resulting in financial savings. Be sure to consult with a tax professional or refer to your country's tax guidelines to understand the specific requirements and benefits.

Engaging in philanthropic activities can also enhance your professional growth and **reputation**. Many companies and employers value corporate social responsibility and community involvement. By actively participating in volunteering or leading philanthropic initiatives, you demonstrate your commitment to making a positive impact and showcase your leadership skills. This can open doors to new career opportunities, networking connections, and potential advancements in your professional life.

Volunteering can also serve as a platform for skill development and career exploration. It allows you to gain practical experience in different areas, such as project management, teamwork, and problem-solving, which are highly transferable to the workplace. Additionally, volunteering in industries or organisations related to your career interests can help you gain firsthand knowledge and insights, enabling you to make informed decisions about your future career path.

Giving back and engaging in philanthropy foster a sense of community and belonging. By actively participating in charitable activities, you connect with like-minded individuals who share your passion for making a positive impact. This sense of community can provide emotional support, networking opportunities, and even mentorship, which can further contribute to your personal and professional growth. Finally, engaging in philanthropy allows you to become an agent of change and contribute to a better world. It allows you to leave a lasting legacy and create a positive ripple effect that extends beyond your immediate sphere of influence.

Conclusion

We have explored a wide range of topics in the realm of financial education, covering foundation basics, savings, spending, debt, investing, the job market, and even the significance of volunteering. Throughout this journey, we have aimed to provide you with the necessary knowledge and tools to navigate the complex world of personal finance and empower you to make informed decisions that will shape your financial future.

First and foremost, we emphasised the importance of mastering the basics of financial literacy. Understanding concepts such as budgeting, saving, and tracking expenses that form the foundation of sound money management. By building a strong financial base, you can lay the groundwork for achieving your short- and long-term financial goals.

We discussed the significance of saving and the power of compounding. Saving is not just about putting money aside for emergencies but also about setting financial goals and working towards them. By cultivating the **habit** of saving, you can create a financial cushion, invest in your future, and enjoy the benefits of financial security and independence.

We also explored the art of responsible spending. Being mindful of your spending habits, distinguishing between needs and wants, and practising conscious consumption are all essential components of maintaining a healthy financial life. By aligning your spending with your values and priorities, you can avoid unnecessary debt, build a strong financial position, and live a more fulfilled life.

Speaking of debt, we delved into strategies for managing and reducing debt. We discussed the importance of understanding different types of debt, exploring options for repayment, and implementing effective debt management strategies. By taking control of your debt, you can alleviate financial stress and free up resources to invest in your future.

Investing, another critical aspect of financial education, was also a focal point. We explored various investment vehicles, from stocks and bonds to commercial property and unit trusts. By understanding the fundamentals of investing and developing a disciplined approach, you can potentially grow your wealth, create passive income streams, and achieve financial freedom over time.

Furthermore, we touched upon the importance of giving back through volunteering. Engaging in charitable activities not only benefits the community but also enriches your own life. Volunteering can provide a sense of purpose, strengthen your social connections, and broaden your perspective on financial well-being. By incorporating philanthropy into your financial journey, you can experience the profound impact of making a difference in the lives of others.

As you conclude this book on financial education, it is essential to remember that financial literacy is a continuous journey. The knowledge and insights you have gained here are just the beginning. The world of finance is ever-evolving, and staying informed and adaptable is crucial. Keep seeking new information, exploring different investment strategies, and staying updated on changing market trends.

Remember to apply the concepts you have learned and track your progress. Regularly review your financial goals, make adjustments as needed, and celebrate your achievements along the way. Financial education is not a one-time event but a lifelong commitment to improving your financial well-being.

Finally, share your knowledge with others. The power of financial education extends beyond personal gain. By sharing what you have learned and encouraging those around you to embark on their own financial journey, you can help create a more financially empowered society.

Thank you for joining us on this enlightening exploration of financial education. Armed with the knowledge and tools presented here, you are now better equipped to navigate the world of personal finance, make informed decisions, and shape a brighter financial future for yourself and those around you. Embrace the journey, stay curious, and continue your pursuit of financial well-being.

Best wishes on your path to financial success!

Timeline of Tips

Birth to Age 5: Introduce Basic Financial Concepts

Teach kids about money, saving, and spending through play.

Use piggy banks or simple savings jars to encourage saving.

Age 6-10: Junior ISA or Savings Account

Consider opening a Junior Individual Savings Account (JISA) to start saving for the child's future.

Encourage regular contributions.

Age 10-12: Open First Bank Account

Introduce children to the concept of a bank account.

Teach them how to deposit and withdraw money.

Age 13-15: Allowance and Budgeting

Give teenagers an allowance to manage.

Teach them budgeting skills, distinguishing between needs and wants.

Age 14-18: Part-Time Jobs and Savings Goals

Encourage part-time work or summer jobs.

Set savings goals for university, ~~a car,~~ or other expenses.

Age 18-21: Build Credit Responsibly

Teach responsible credit card usage and its impact on credit scores.

Discuss the importance of maintaining good credit.

Age 18-25: University Savings or Student Loans

Start saving for college education or discuss student loan options.

Explore scholarship opportunities.

Age 22-30: Build Emergency Fund & House Deposit

Emphasize the importance of an emergency fund.

Aim to save at least three to six months' worth of living expenses.

Contribute to Lifetime ISA (LISA) to maximise first house deposit.

Age 25+: Retirement Accounts (Pensions).

Begin contributing to employer-sponsored retirement plans.

Consider opening a Personal Pension.

Age 25-30: Debt Management.

Develop a strategy for paying down any outstanding debts (e.g., student loans, credit cards).

Age 30-35: Saving for Major Life Events.

Start saving for significant life events like a wedding, buying a home, or having children.

Age 35-40: Review Insurance Needs.

Evaluate life insurance, illness cover and health insurance.

Adjust policies as necessary.

Age 40+: Maximize Retirement Contributions.

Increase contributions to retirement accounts as income grows.

Explore catch-up contributions for retirement savings.

Age 45-50: Estate Planning.

Begin estate planning, including wills and trusts.

Appoint guardians for minor children if needed.

Age 50-55: University Funding for Children.

Evaluate college savings progress and adjust as necessary.

Research scholarships and financial aid options.

Age 55-65: Retirement Transition Plan.

Develop a retirement transition plan, including anticipated expenses and lifestyle changes.

Consider working part time.

Age 65+: Retirement Lifestyle and Withdrawal Strategy.

Create a retirement budget and withdrawal strategy for your pension.

Consider downsizing or relocating for retirement.

Age 70+: Long-Term Care and Estate Distribution.

Investigate long-term care insurance options.

Update estate plans and distribution preferences.

Throughout Life:

Financial Education and Review.

Continuously educate yourself on financial topics.

Regularly review and adjust your financial plan to meet changing goals and circumstances.

Money Matters Sorted

About the Author

Daniel Jones is a financial adviser, not an author. He talks to people about money everyday and is often surprised with dismissive views individuals have for their personal finances.

With a bit of help from AI, he has written this book to help the younger generation understand the importance of their money and how it should be used.

He is a passionate advocate of people taking control of their finances and always look to promote the importance of financial education. He believes that by instilling a solid foundation of financial understanding at an early age, individuals can make confident and informed decisions, avoid common pitfalls, and achieve long-term financial well-being.

He lives in Cardiff, is a father to two young children and husband to Clare.

You can contact him via:

his website:	www.moneymatterssorted.co.uk
email:	moneymatterssorted@gmail.com
Twitter (X):	@danelfyn

www.ingramcontent.com/pod-product-compliance
Lightning Source LLC
Chambersburg PA
CBHW070201230526
45471CB00002B/760